HAS THE ECUMENICAL MOVEMENT A FUTURE?

Has The Ecumenical Movement A Future?

WILLEM VISSER 't HOOFT

CHRISTIAN JOURNALS LIMITED
BELFAST

First English edition 1974 by Christian Journals Limited,
10 Brand's Arcade, Belfast BT1 5FG

ISBN 0 904302 00 8

Translated from the Dutch by Annebeth Mackie

Cover by Blaise Levai

Made and Printed in Ireland by
Cahill & Co, Dublin

CONTENTS

FOREWORD

'Has the Ecumenical Movement a Future?' The question is not simply a rhetorical one. The whole complex of inter-church relationships which has come to be called the ecumenical movement, is under attack from some quarters and suffers from simply being ignored in others. That the ecumenical movement has a past is in no small measure due to Dr Visser 't Hooft. More than anyone else still living, he is a personal link with those pioneers of whom he speaks in Chapter I. There the four periods of ecumenical history are analysed, not as so often by a tedious repetition of the history of a string of conferences, but by picking out the leading ideas of each phase, exemplified in the men who expounded and lived by them—John R. Mott, Bishop Charles Brent, Archbishop William Temple, among the giants of the early days.

As an honorary President of the World Council of Churches, Dr Visser 't Hooft is part of the present. In these pages he shows the characteristic, familiar to those who know him, of being able to understand swiftly the convictions of those with whom he disagrees and to evaluate afresh the positions which time has changed and is changing. He makes some shrewd comments on features in the contemporary ecumenical scene. There is an anti-institutional temper abroad which needs to be self-critical as it begins to harden into its own institutional patterns. There is a confusion about words like 'dialogue' in which valid meanings for a christian must be distinguished from those to be rejected. Even in so brief a compass, I could wish that he had paid more attention to the question of the form which the Church must take if its unity is to be evident without its freedom being impaired. It is a subject on which the Faith and Order Movement continues to be fruitful.

What of the future? Dr Visser 't Hooft rightly repudiates in his introduction the notion that he is casting a horoscope. But he does ask the questions which the ecumenical movement must face if it is to regain some lost loyalties and capture new ones. In a world where white westerners are a minority, some of us have got to become accustomed to finding the agenda being drawn up on lines which are unfamiliar and even uncongenial. I am glad that readers of English can now join in this enquiry, along with the readers of Dutch, to whom the lectures were first addressed. We are part, though not as we tend to think necessarily the dominant part, of a world which 'writes the agenda for the Church' only in the sense that it is the world which God so loved that He gave His Son, to whose redeeming work the ecumenical movement exists to witness. If it does not, it should not have a future.

Oliver Bristol:

INTRODUCTION

I hope that this title does not raise any false expectations. It might be that people hope to find an answer here to the question what will the ecumenical movement look like twenty or thirty years from now. That however is a question which no one can answer. When I ask myself how I visualized the future in 1930, or in 1940, or 1950 or 1960, then I must admit that things have always gone differently from my expectations. There is therefore no point in adding to the number of incorrect pictures of the future—thus giving more food for ridicule to later generations. In any case, there are too many facile prophecies concerning the future of the church and Christianity.

It is my intention to make a contribution to the conversation about the road which the ecumenical movement should take in order truly to have a future. A choice must be made between all sorts of possibilities. There are some roads which come to a dead end, there are others which lead to a goal. We have to ask ourselves which is the road which is indicated to us.

Of course I can only speak from my own personal conviction. And I am aware that it is at the same time an advantage and a handicap that I belong to the older generation, which has been involved in the ecumenical movement for a very long time. An advantage because the experience which has been gained over all these years must have some weight in the decisions which have to be taken today. A handicap because I may, rightly, be accused of attaching too much importance to the past.

THE FOUR PERIODS OF ECUMENICAL HISTORY

No one will be surprised if I start with a look back over the past of the ecumenical movement. As one of the very few who had the privilege of taking part in this history for fifty years, I can only speak from inside this history. There is every reason to ask ourselves what really did happen during those years. There is a great deal of ignorance and misunderstanding about the early development; a great many mistakes are made which could be avoided by drawing the conclusions from earlier experience.

Obviously I am not concerned with listing facts about conferences and assemblies, but rather with the history of the prevailing motives and insights. Very little thorough work has been done in this field. What I am offering therefore is an attempt to give some sort of survey of ecumenical history by identifying the convictions which have given the movement its particular character.

Though we are concerned with a period of about sixty years, there have been radical changes during that time. Distinctions between the various periods must therefore be drawn up. Such distinctions are always open to question. We all know that historians can never agree whether the Middle Ages and the Renaissance or the Reformation and the Enlightenment can really be considered as periods which can be clearly distinguished from each other. I do not maintain therefore that my distinctions are the only valid ones. I think however that by distinguishing four periods it becomes easier to understand the development as well as the present situation. I have therefore chosen the following division: 1910 to 1934, 1934 to 1948, 1948 to 1960 and 1960 up to a date which still lies in the future Clearly these dates have no absolute significance; inevitably the periods overlap to some extent.

The First Period

The first period, beginning with the World Missionary Conference in Edinburgh in 1910 and ending in 1934 with the preparations by J.H. Oldham for the Oxford Conference of 1937, could be called, with an allusion to one of Pirandello's plays: 'Various ecumenical groups in search of a theme for the ecumenical movement'. This is a period in which ecumenical initiatives were taken on many sides and in many places. Their common factor was the desire to release the churches from their isolation and to bring them to some form of community. But they point in different directions.

To a great extent this is due to the fact that each of these groups was strongly dominated by the personality of its founder. The International Missionary Council and the World Student Christian Federation emanated from John R. Mott, Faith and Order from Charles Brent, Life and Work from Nathan Söderblom.

John R. Mott was the arch-pioneer—he was the first to survey world events with one strategic glance and systematically set to work in order to combine all the forces which were necessary for a world mission. The titles of his books sound like clarion calls: 'Strategic points in the World's Conquest', 'The Evangelization of the World in this generation', 'The Decisive Hour of Christian Mission'. And in his countless journeys his life really took on universal dimensions, encircling the globe. The ecumenical movement was for him one great working and living community of all those who wanted to bring the Gospel to every corner of the earth. His sense of proportion did not admit theological or ecclesiastical differences as obstacles to the fulfilment of this central task. In 1910 he succeeded in laying the foundations of the International Missionary Council.

Charles Brent was another missionary. He was however of the opinion that the divisions between the churches do not only obstruct co-operation, but that they also obscure the truth of the Gospel of reconciliation. He became the apostle of the visible unity of the churches. No matter how insurmountable the obstacles, we must try to reach agreement on the questions of faith and order. All the churches must be involved in this effort. The Ecumenical Patriarchate in Constantinople lent a willing ear, but the invitation to the Vatican was declined politely but firmly. The Faith and Order Movement called the churches together and the first world conference in Lausanne substantiated the hope of possible progress along the road to unity.

Nathan Söderblom learnt in the Christian youth movement to believe in the unity of all Christians, but this was precisely the reason for his suffering when in 1914 the churches of the belligerent countries identified themselves to a great extent with the national interest, so that they preached and prayed *against* each other. The real aim should be to serve together. It should not be necessary to wait for agreement on dogmatic questions in order to 'Live' and 'Work' together so that the great moral, social and international questions can be tackled together. The conference in Stockholm, where Söderblom's prophetic vision predominated, opened up new horizons.

We have therefore three movements which respectively considered the apostolate, the catholicity and the 'diaconia' as the basis of the ecumenical ideal, and which each recruited their own supporters. The situation was complicated still further by the deadlock which developed in the theological conversations: the Anglo-Saxon side was dominated by an activist theology of the social gospel which, from a blind faith in the progress of mankind, believed roughly speaking in the possibility of the short term abolition of sin in social and international life; while this was opposed from the German side by the theology of the two kingdoms, originating in a deep-seated pessimism and an atmosphere of the *'Untergang des Abendlandes'* (The decline of the West), in which it seemed impossible to find any point of contact between the Kingdom of God and the kingdom of this world.

The great conferences of Edinburgh, Stockholm, Lausanne and Jerusalem had raised high hopes. For it was no small matter that the churches, after so many centuries of isolation, were again entering into conversation with each other. Would the churches be able to give a spiritual basis to the new internationalism? Would they be able to act as conscience to the still extremely vulnerable League of Nations? These were the prevailing hopes and questions.

When the great financial-economic depression came in 1929 with its catastrophic consequences, when new and acute international conflicts developed which the League was unable to solve, there also developed a crisis in the ecumenical movement. The worst of it was not that the financial situation of the various organizations, already in a weak position, was crippled. The worst was that the enthusiasm which had been generated proved to have no strong roots. It became clear that the movement was too dependent on the international tides of politics and culture. There were too many people who had joined the ecumenical army because they judged that the market trend was in favour of co-operation, internationalism and tolerance, who now left the army because it became clear that this trend was beginning to change. The real crisis therefore was an identity-crisis. The aims of the ecumenical movement were not clear. Was it based on a deeper understanding of the return of the Christ. Dietrich Bonhoeffer wrote in 1932 that the prevailing confusion of thought was due to the fact that the fundamental theological questions as to the real meaning of the new encounter between the churches had never been tackled properly. I myself wrote in 1934 that the much discussed ecumenical

15

crisis was of such serious, and perhaps even fatal, dimensions precisely because it took place in an atmosphere of acute inner uncertainty. In view of the fact that we hear so much of the 'ecumenical crisis' in recent years, it might be useful to recall that there was a similar crisis about forty years ago.

The Second Period

We now arrive at the second period which begins in 1934. This was the year in which the ecumenical movement was confronted by the Church struggle in Germany, and in which Life and Work, under the leadership of J.H. Oldham, made concrete plans for the spiritual preparation of the churches for the resistance against the totalitarian ideologies.

The central question of the meeting in Fanö (Denmark) was whether Life and Work should choose sides in the struggle in Germany between the recently formed Confessing Churches on the one hand, and the so-called German Christians, who were supported by the Nazi government, on the other. One group held that the ecumenical movement should take up an entirely neutral position in such a situation. But George Bell, Bishop of Chichester, who had kept himself closely informed by Dietrich Bonhoeffer, realized that the Confessing Church was defending central Christian principles, on the validity of which depended the existence of the whole ecumenical movement. In the end the meeting expressed itself both in word and in deed for the encouragement of the Confessing Church.

The outlines of the ecumenical movement thus began to take on a clearer form. Adolf Hitler and his henchmen, such as Rosenburg who attacked the ecumenical movement fiercely, did the great service of presenting a challenge which the movement could not afford to ignore. J.H. Oldham, the first secretary of the International Missionary Council was deeply convinced that this answer could only be forthcoming if the churches mobilized all their forces—not just the theologians but especially also the laymen. He therefore sacrificed his work for his beloved Missionary Council for the time being, in order to devote all his energies to the preparation of the next world conference of Life and Work in Oxford, which would of course concentrate on the task of the church as regards the community and the state. The ecumenical situation was beginning to clarify. The possibility of a common witness about the acute problems was taking shape.

The theological development pointed in the same direction. It was a period of theological renaissance. About 1930 Karl Barth began to acquire a world-wide reputation. But there were many others who made their own contribution: Niebuhr, Emil Brunner, Paul Tillich, Nicholas Berdyaev. The inner cohesion of the Bible was rediscovered by such men as Hoskyns, Schniewind and C.H. Dodd. Thus biblical theology acquired a worldwide influence through Hendrik Kraemer's book for the Madras conference of 1938. In this connection the church also regained its biblical dignity. Karl Barth, who began in the manner of Kierkegaard by describing the life of the church as a great betrayal of the Gospel, called his new work on dogmatics 'Kirchliche Dogmatik' in 1932. In 1934 Berkelbach van der Sprenkel wrote that over against a purely sociological view of the church, an awareness was emerging with a renewed conviction that between all kinds of human community there is a communion which is based on another foundation, which is the covenant of God with his people. This was the spiritual atmosphere in which the plan was born to establish a World Council of Churches in which the churches themselves could have the responsibility for the fulfilment of their ecumenical task.

The threat of war and the war itself gave the ecumenical movement the great opportunity to prove that the movement towards unity of Christians was not just a by-product of a worldly internationalism, but drew its strength from the very essence of the church. A few weeks before the war the world conference of Christ in Youth in Amsterdam expressed this simply and correctly: 'The nations and peoples of the world are drifting apart, the churches are coming together... In war, conflict or persecution, we must strengthen one another and preserve our Christian unity unbroken.' During the war years many people based their lives on this conviction. Even though there was only a minimum of direct contact or because the absence of contact created a stronger desire for fellowship, the feeling of Christian solidarity penetrated deeper into their hearts. During this period the World Council of Churches grew in spite of all opposition.

During this time there were many thoughts and

dreams of a postwar world which would return to Christianity after this great physical and spiritual catastrophe, and which would seek inspiration in Christian insights. Already before the war J.H. Oldham had unceasingly stressed that Western civilization could only be saved through a re-discovery of the central Christian truth. The poet T.S. Eliot, who belonged to J.H. Oldham's circle of wise men, published his 'Idea of a Christian Society' during the first weeks of the war. In a number of resistance movements such as 'Vrij Nederland' (Free Netherlands), 'Trouw' (True), in the Netherlands; 'Témoignage chrétien' (Christian Witness) in France; and the Kreisau Circle in Germany, there lived the hope that the churches would be able to fill the great spiritual vacuum and give form to a new society. Dietrich Bonhoeffer too, during his last years, thought along these lines. In his 'Ethik' (Ethics) he wrote imposing pages on the cultural values, humanity, reason, liberty, human rights which had become independent because it was believed that they could maintain themselves without the church, or even over against the church, but which were now, in the great chaos, turning back to the church as their real mother. Only under the protection of Christ can civilization lead a real life. In 1943, when Bonhoeffer was already in prison, he still wrote about the reconstruction of the inner and exterior life of the nations on the basis of Christianity. This is the Bonhoeffer, rather than the Bonhoeffer of 1944, who was typical of the ecumenical atmosphere of those years. During that period many reports were completed by us in the World Council, which were based on the assumption that after the war the churches would have unprecedented chances to exercise a decisive influence on the pattern of the post-war social and international order. This was not a matter of power politics for the church. The basic concern was that the church would at long last resume her responsibility in and for our culture.

The Third Period

The third period begins in 1948 when the World Council of Churches was at last officially instituted at Amsterdam. No longer a pipedream, the Council now had to learn to live in and with the prosaic realities of church-life. During these post-war years a great deal of hard work was done for renewal both in the Church and in the world, but at the same time there was a strong tendency—after the time of nihilism and chaos—to look for security and to go back to the trusted traditions. Moreover, these were the years of the cold war, when almost everyone was expected to choose sides. Many problems faced the young World Council during this time. Pressures from all sides attempted to enlist the ecumenical movement for this or that ecclesiastical or secular political side. Nor was the frontline as clearly marked as in the days of national socialism. The Council's own policy had to be traced out in the midst of all these tensions. It proved to be a time for both consolidation and expansion, when the ecumenical movement enjoyed a favourable wind because it was generally felt that in the fragile conditions of the post-war world there was need of a movement which attempted to mobilize the whole of Christianity for the task of spiritual and material reconstruction, and which thought and acted in terms of the universal categories of the whole church for the whole world. The ecumenical concept was able to penetrate into many churches which up till then had held themselves aloof from the movement. Every theologian of importance began to take part in the ecumenical conversation. Even Karl Barth, who before the war had been extremely critical in his attitude, gave his vigorous assistance. Someone at Amsterdam, in 1948, said: 'My whole theological library seems to be at this meeting'. For the preparation of the second Assembly at Evanston the Council was able to enlist the co-operation of nearly all the theologians and laymen who were then indicating the new directions.

There was a considerable measure of theological agreement. The Bible had ceased to be the book which had better remain closed because it could only cause disagreement about its correct interpretation—it now became the book which we could open together in order to discover the contents of our common task.

The church continued to occupy a central position in the ecumenical sphere of thought. But it was the renewed church, the people of God who are ever being re-formed. Many countries and churches saw the development of lay-movements such as the impressive *Kirchentag* (Churchweek) in Germany, and under the leadership of Hendrik Kraemer the

Ecumenical Institute at Bossey became a source of inspiration to these movements. Considerable efforts were made to promote church unity—at first with great expectations. In 1947 the Church of South India was born; and after this union of the Episcopal, Presbyterian and Methodist traditions, there would surely be many other reunions which would follow on after this breakthrough. But unity was not pursued just for the sake of unity. The tasks which could only be fulfilled through co-operation and mutual assistance must be accepted together and carried out with a common mind. These tasks included mission, service and prophetic witness to the world. This meant that the walls of partition between the International Missionary Council and the World Council of Churches must now finally be pulled down. This integration was intended as an indication that the Church cannot live without mission and evangelism—that mission was synonymous with the building up of the church. By organizing the diaconal task on a worldwide basis the ecumenical movement made it clear that it did not only believe in the solidarity of all Christians, but also in solidarity with all who suffer from want.

There was a strong awareness that the church must be the watchman who proclaims the Word of God which points the way for nations and for humanity. This carried with it the implication that the World Council should, not just incidentally but constantly, not just as a matter of principle, but in concrete ways, concern itself with the important social and international questions of the day. The concept of a 'Responsible Society' was elaborated, not as an alternative system, but as a criterion and touchstone. All the existing structures were critically examined from this point of view. Through the growing participation of Asia and Africa the third world came to occupy the centre of attention.

A great number of economists and politicians was drawn into the studies concerned with the rapid social change in Asia and Africa. In this field, but more particularly in the work of the Commission of the Churches on International Affairs, the chief problem was the position which the Church ought to take in the cold war between the political West and the political East. The World Council refused to let itself be used by one or other of the power-policies—in spite of all the sympathy which it lost that way. There were tense moments in the relations between the East Europeans and the Western churches—at the times of the war in Korea, the Hungarian crisis—but the community was not broken. Thus the way was paved for the conversations with the Russian Orthodox Church which began at the time of the Second Assembly at Evanston (1954).

The Fourth Period

The fourth period in the development of the ecumenical movement begins in 1960. Why that year? At first sight it does not look like a year of transition. It was the year in which the International Missionary

Council and the World Council of Churches met in Edinburgh to commemorate the fact that half a century earlier the ecumenical movement had started in the same place. There was a general feeling that by continuing along the chosen road, the movement would increase in strength. The preparations for the integration of the Missionary Council and the World Council had reached a satisfactory result. The churches in East Asia had come together in a regional organization, thus indicating the important role which the churches in the third world were assuming in the ecumenical life. Long conversations with the Russian Orthodox Church had achieved that this church was now prepared to become a member of the World Council. It was also the year in which Pope John XXIII reached the decision to set up the Secretariat for Unity and in which the first official conversation between the Vatican and the World Council took place. At the Assembly of 1961 in New Delhi I could therefore speak of a general ecumenical mobilization. It looked as if a time of full flowering and great harvests had come for the ecumenical movement and for the World Council of Churches, as if we were on the right road, so that all we had to do was to march straight on.

And yet there were even at that time all sorts of phenomena which did not fit into this oversimplified picture, and which indicated that a great change of weather was imminent. As usual, it began with the young people. The World Student Christian Federation held an extremely well prepared world conference in Strasbourg in 1960. The plan was to make it a teaching conference in order to pass on to the new generation, the insights which had been gained in the ecumenical conversation of the last ten or twenty years. The theme was to be 'The Life and Mission of the Church'. In a bulky publication the students were told what lessons could be drawn from the history of Church and mission, for the future task of missions. The speakers who had been invited were men who had taken an active part in the ecumenical movement over a great number of years, such as D.T. Niles, Lesslie Newbigin and myself. Karl Barth also came in order to take part in a conversation with the delegates. However, the course which the conference took was entirely different from that which had been anticipated by the leaders. There was no real contact between the speakers and the audience. The article on offer did not meet the demand. It was not clear what the students were in fact looking for, but the reaction to the heavy stress on church and mission was in any case a negative one. 'What is the connection', they asked suspiciously, 'between the ideal church you refer to, and the church institutions which we have got to know?'. And they wanted to learn more about the world. An astute student leader remarked: 'They don't want high churchmanship, but high worldmanship'. In the following years it became clear that this was more than a student whim. The entire theological situation was changing rapidly. The opinion that 'Karl Barth has had his day' was repeated over and over again, thus providing an excellent excuse for the younger generation to leave the thick volumes of the

'Kirchliche Dogmatik' unopened. A great stir was caused by Bishop Robinson's book 'Honest to God', in which an attempt is made to restore an immanent, horizontally aimed theology. And the appearance of Vahanian's book 'The death of God' sparked off the much publicized discussion whether, and in what sense, we should speak of the death of God. Does this mean the end of an era in which the majority of men took faith in God more or less for granted? Or does it mean that modern man has become impervious to any belief in God? Of the great men who had dominated theology for thirty years, there remained only Paul Tillich and especially Dietrich Bonhoeffer, whose reputation now began to spread over the whole world, based almost exclusively on the tentative ideas written down in prison in 1944, in the later letters—about modern man who has come of age and who is without religion, and about the importance for the Church to turn towards the world. Another radical shift in ideas took place in the field of Bible study. The scholars were pointing out how many different traditions were represented in the Bible, thus putting a query behind the biblical theology of the earlier generation which had been based on the fundamental unity of the biblical *kerygma*.

And what of the church? Who would now dare speak of the 'Century of the Church' as people were wont to do in the 'twenties? Anyway, what had happened to the renewal of the Church? Had it not just remained, in the phrase of Peter Berger's books of 1961, a 'noise of solemn assemblies'? Had the Church not succumbed after all to the temptation to become a part of the successful establishment? Were the sociologists not right when they maintained that the Church is just an institution which is automatically subject to the rigid laws which apply to all institutionalized social phenomena and therefore bent on self-perpetuation, and intolerant of or immune from any radical renewal?

In view of all this it is quite natural that the ecumenical movement and the World Council of Churches are regarded quite differently. Is it still possible to maintain that the ecumenical movement can indicate a new road? Is it not true that the World Council itself has become an institution? Moreover, has it not put the Church far too much in the centre? Is the original meaning of the world 'ecumenical' not *world*-wide?

Is there not, behind the social and international thinking of the World Council, the illusion that the Church will yet again, as of old, be able to dominate the whole of society? Have we really finished with the Western Christian imperialist complex, or must we conclude—from Western politics, from missionary behaviour, from the attitude towards the race problem—that Western Christians are still convinced of their superiority and their predestination to be the leaders of all mankind? Has the time not come, so younger people ask, to reject the way of reform which is mainly concerned to eradicate the worst excesses of the present system, and to summon all Christians to work for a radical revolution? Surely the real intention of the Gospel is to bring about a total change in the relations between classes, races and nations in the light of the dawning of the Kingdom of God?

Every position which before 1960 had come to be considered as an established conviction thus became in recent years the subject of queries. The consensus which had been reached on many points lost its validity, and we are forced to start the painful rebuilding of a new consensus. This is painful because many churches are undergoing a process of polarization in which the different positions are becoming ever more fiercely opposed to each other. On the one hand are those who have been so shocked by the extreme conclusions arrived at by the supporters of the new direction that they even refuse to listen to the very valid questions which have been raised. On the other side there are the people who are so fascinated by the novelty of the questions which assail them that they feel that the insights gained by previous generations can no longer have any real meaning for them.

We thus find ourselves in an extremely complicated ecumenical situation. The traditional differences between the denominations continue to exist. But they are crossed by trans-denominational dividing lines, so that people in one denomination come to be opposed to one another and stand on the same side as people from another denomination. Is it possible for the churches to have ecumenical relationships with each other, while they are struggling with deep divisions among their own members? What is the point of a conversation between the churches where there is hardly a church which can say that it represents one single particular theological position? And besides all this there are the Eastern Orthodox Churches which have had to fight for their lives, and the many young churches in Asia and Africa which are fully occupied with the task of evangelism, which are not really interested in the new problems and which fail to understand why the ecumenical movement cannot continue along the same road. Not long ago, when I visited Russia and Indonesia, I had the feeling that my audience was wondering what 'these agitated Westerners had found to worry about now?'. And for people of my generation it is sometimes easier to feel at home in theological discussions in Asia or Africa than at such discussions in Europe or America.

To keep all the disparate elements together has therefore become even more difficult than before. At times it feels as if we are no longer contemporaries. Some people still speak entirely as if they are still in what I have here called the second and third periods; others already seem to have got into a fifth period, of which the contours can only be dimly discerned.

For those who possess even the least little bit of ecumenical feeling, one thing is clear; we must let go of each other. And that means we must listen to each other. To let the polarization continue to escalate unhindered, or to accept it without protest would be to belie the ecumenical movement—not just the ecumenical institutions, but the fellowship which we have found in Christ. We must therefore enter into the problems and accept the challenges of today, but not without gratitude for that which we have received

29

from the history of the ecumenical movement.

In the next three chapters I will therefore make an attempt to answer those central questions which dominate the present ecumenical discussion. These questions are:

— Is the ecumenical movement suffering from institutional paralysis?

— Should we replace mission as it has been practised up till now by a dialogue with the other religions?

— Should the ecumenical movement follow the agenda of the Church—or the agenda of the world?

IS THE ECUMENICAL MOVEMENT SUFFERING FROM INSTITUTIONAL PARALYSIS?

The criticism most frequently levelled at the ecumenical movement is that it has landed itself in a blind alley by being too closely linked with churches which have themselves lost their dynamism and become immobile, self-assertive institutions. A World Council of Churches dependent in the last analysis on the churches is, the argument runs, itself condemned to travel the same hopeless road of institutionalism. There are already clear signs, so it is said, that the invigorating pioneer spirit of the early days of the World Council is fast vanishing and the decline into bureaucracy far advanced. What hope can still be invested in an ecumenical organization which is simply another cog in the ecclesiastical machine?

To this I say that we need to distinguish between two different attitudes to this issue. Some people regard any attempt to give the Christian fellowship institutional form as a departure from or a betrayal of the Gospel. Others, while convinced that in this world community life of any sort requires some institutional forms, believe at the same time that the Church must always guard against the tendency of institutional forms to claim autonomy and must see to it that these forms continue to be subordinate to the Church's permanent task, and therefore to the Holy Spirit who reforms and renews the Church.

A radical anti-institutional tendency has accompanied the Church throughout its history. It may already be seen, perhaps, in the attitude of the protomartyr Stephen. In his presentation of history, the official religious leaders 'always' (Acts 7:51) resisted the Holy Spirit and persecuted the true prophets. In the Middle Ages the most influential and most interesting representative of this opposition to the official Church was the abbot Joachim of Fiore. He believed that the Old Testament dispensation of God the Father and the New Testament of God the Son and the hierarchical Church would be followed by a third dispensation, that of God the Holy Spirit. In this third dispensation there would no longer be any place for church organization of any kind; complete spiritual freedom would be the order of the day. Ignazio Silone, the former Marxist, wrote a splendid little book about Pope Celestine V, a strange Pope, strongly influenced by Joachim, who discovered after a few unhappy months that you could not long remain Pope if you really believed the Church to be an obstacle to the Holy Spirit. Silone puts it in these words: 'God created souls, not institutions. Souls are immortal: institutions, kingdoms, armies, churches and governments are not.'

At the end of the seventeenth century we find a whole chorus of voices in Europe, and especially in Holland, declaring that the official churches represented a corruption of genuine Christianity. Gottfried Arnold's 'Impartial History of Churches and Heresies' (1699) is a typical example. It was not all that impartial, however, its thesis being that the churches were always wrong and the heretics always right.

Coming much closer to our own times, there was

Søren Kierkegaard. In his campaign to have the Gospel taken with full seriousness he opposed the Danish State Church even to the point of maintaining that merely to take part in its services was to commit grievous sin. Not to participate in its life was at least to refrain from mocking God.

Tolstoy arrived at the same conclusion, if for other reasons. The New Testament condemned violence outright; the State was based on violence; the Church accepted and supported the State. Therefore, he argued, 'The churches are anti-Christian institutions'. I can still recall how deeply this argument impressed me when I was in the sixth form.

Do we not also have to mention Emil Brunner in this context? Certainly he had no wish to do away with the Church. Yet he believed that what we call the church is something very different from what the New Testament means by the *Ecclesia*. And the difference is precisely this, that the original Christian community was a pure communion of persons and in no sense an institution.

It is widely held today that any institutional form is a betrayal of the original intention of the Gospel. This view links up with all kinds of anarchistic elements in contemporary thinking about society and government. Michael Bakunin, the father of anarchism, had already described the State as the Church's younger brother. The Church is seen as part of the fixed order of things, part of the notorious 'establishment'. Anyone who wants to overthrow this order must also settle accounts with the Church, since the Church undergirds it. In the so-called 'counter-culture' which has emerged in radical intellectual circles and especially among young people, all repressive powers, the Church included, are under attack. Where religious elements play any part in this culture at all they tend to work not in favour of the Church but in the direction of movements outside or hostile to the Church.

We should not be too quick to dismiss this challenge. The complete rejection of institutional forms touches a responsive chord in all of us. Only the most inveterate of clerics could fail to be saddened by the torpidity and the resistance to real renewal so often encountered in the Church. Which of us has not dreamed of a fellowship relieved of all organizational junk, a fellowship which would live in real freedom, responding spontaneously and without regimentation to the inspiration of the Holy Spirit?

Yet the complete rejection of the institution is surely impracticable. Not because it would be too risky to abandon the Church's existing order without knowing what would take its place but for a much more fundamental reason. It is simply untrue to say that the community we meet in the New Testament is a purely charismatic fellowship, one which lives only by the inspiration of the Holy Spirit. Certainly the gifts of the Spirit are indispensable. But this does not mean that the Church can manage without rules and agreed arrangements for its common life. Certainly the gifts of the Spirit are indispensable. But this does mean that the Church can manage without rules and agreed arrangements for its common life.

Certainly the Church is the people of God, but as such it is made up of imperfect human beings who can only live together if certain limits are imposed on their behaviour. The people of God live in this world and in order to perform their function in this world and in order to find their proper form. This means that institutional elements have been there in the Church from the very beginning. And this remains true throughout history. It is characteristic that even groups and sects which protest against the institutional church themselves acquire institutional traits. Emil Brunner refers to the YMCA, missionary societies, and Moral Rearmament as examples of non-institutional fellowships which are more akin to the New Testament *Ecclesia*. But anyone who knows these movements is aware that they too have had to cope with the problems of leadership, discipline and standards of mutual conduct, although in different ways, and have therefore not been exempt from the problems of the religious institution.

Monica Wilson, the sociologist who has made a study of the independent sects in Africa, describes how groups which rebelled against the old structures have themselves had to devise new structures. Her conclusion is that Christians who think that every religious organization is destined to wither away are just as mistaken as Karl Marx was in making a similar prediction about the State.

There is, however, another criticism of church institutionalism which is certainly well-founded, based as it is on the truth that while structure, order, and even law all have their legitimate place in the life of the Church, every order carries with it at the same time serious dangers. For what Nietzsche said about the State can equally be said of every other institution: 'It wants to be an important animal.' Human institutions have an inherent tendency to self-assertiveness and empire-building and thus to become an end in themselves rather than a means. The real question is therefore whether it is possible so to guide and control the institutional element that it continues to play a subservient role to the task which the Lord has assigned to His Church.

It is significant that Karl Barth, who at first attacked every form of institutionalism in the Church, as Kierkegaard had done, later reached the conclusion that it was a mistake to think we had to choose between a church imprisoned in institutional armour and a church devoid of all order and discipline. The Church has its own distinctive way: namely the use of institutional means in obedience to Christ. A church which wishes to be purely spiritual runs the risk of losing its own identity and becoming the mere plaything of secular forces. The real struggle, therefore, is not against the institutional element as such but against its tendency to claim first place. When the institution dominates, there is no real possibility of conversion and renewal. To quote the Dutch professor Gunning, it is the Church's resistance to conversion which is the root of all our troubles.

How does all this apply to the ecumenical movement? It means that it is irrelevant to ask whether the ecumenical movement needs an institutional form, the decisive question is whether the institutional factors in the ecumenical movement are a law unto themselves.

People sometimes speak as if in the year 1937 the ecumenical movement suffered a fall from grace, so to speak. Up to that point the argument goes, the ecumenical movement had been a free, unregulated, spontaneously flourishing movement, with the pioneers defending its independence from ecclesiastical institutions. But then the churches saw their chance to take charge of this movement, to found the World Council of Churches, and in this way to make sure that the movement ceased to be a threat and a nuisance in the life of the churches.

This is, of course, a complete travesty of the historical facts. The idea that around about 1937 there was a conspiracy on the part of ecclesiastical leaders to clericalize a spontaneous unofficial church movement is simply a legend. The fact is that the pioneers, the men who gave the movement its impetus, were the very people who from the beginning wanted to draw the churches into the movement. John R. Mott worked strenuously to enlist the support of reluctant church leaders, such as the then Archbishop of Canterbury, for the first World Missionary Council. His devoted colleague J.H. Oldham was already speaking about a future 'League of Churches' at the time of the founding of the International Missionary Council in 1920. In 1910 Bishop Charles Brent founded the Faith and Order Movement as an organization for dialogue between the churches. As early as 1919 Nathan Söderblom was trying to kindle enthusiasm for the establishment of a genuinely representative world council of churches. In 1920 Archbishop Germanos of Thyatira helped to draft the 'Ecyclical Letter' of the Patriarch of Constantinople proposing the establishment of a *koinonia*, an instrument of fellowship, of the churches. The really remarkable thing is that the churches at first wanted little to do with such plans. It took twenty years for the situation to ripen sufficiently to persuade the churches to act. It was precisely in ecclesiastical circles that there was a feeling that the ecumenical movement could become a considerable nuisance if the churches themselves had to assume responsibility for it.

The man who, by his vision, wisdom and tenacity, contributed more than anyone to the creation of the World Council of Churches was J.H. Oldham, a layman with a deep interest in theology, a man of the missionary movement but who held no official church function. If we ask what his deepest motives were, it is quite clear that the very last thing he wanted was to shunt the ecumenical movement into the sidings of ecclesiastical institutionalism. On the contrary, his major concern was that the ecumenical movement should liberate the churches from their egocentricity and mobilize them for their new tasks in a new world. All this can be found in the detailed study on 'The Function of the Church in Society' which he wrote for the Oxford Conference of 1937. Oldham was profoundly impressed by the radical crisis of Western civilization. Far more dangerous than the threat of atheistic or pagan ideology was the fact that the traditionally Christian countries could offer no alternative. Did the churches not see that it was not a matter of saving their own skins but of making visible on the basis of the Gospel the outlines of a different and renewed society?

This entailed a task of gigantic historical dimensions, one which could only be carried out by mobilizing all available creative resources. Oldham tried to entice the theologians and philosophers out of their studies. Like Socrates he sought to play the role of midwife assisting at the birth of new insights. But intellectual effort was not enough. The situation was so critical that at the same time work had to be done on the practical application and communication of new insights. It was here that Oldham reached a far-reaching decision. He chose the churches. This was a far from obvious thing to do. Oldham saw very clearly the inadequacy of the churches and made no secret of it. He was deeply dissatisfied with the status quo in the churches. But he also had the courage to affirm that the church of Christ is the *only* hope for the world. The churches with all their frailty and disobedience were still to him the representatives of the people of God called and gathered afresh by Christ again and again in human history, and in these churches the true church is constantly being reborn.

Not surprisingly, it was not the laity who displayed the greatest resistance to this vision but a few clerically minded church leaders. Led by Dr Headlam, the Bishop of Gloucester, they opposed the plan to establish a World Council of Churches, because such a council would also concern itself with social and political matters. They wanted an ecumenical movement dealing exclusively with questions of faith and order. But Oldham's vision carried the day. It is quite clear from the plan drawn up in 1937 that the object in founding the World Council was to help the churches to act responsibly and to bear clear witness in the modern world.

What I have said so far, however, does not sufficiently answer the question of the institutionalization of the ecumenical movement. For even assuming that the foundation of the World Council was not intended as an ecclesiastical take-over of the ecumenical movement, it could still be the case that the actual, if unintended result of the decision in 1937 was to change a dynamic movement into an institution which brought the existing situation between the churches to a standstill. Where today is the splendid vision of a united and renewed Christendom which gave so much courage and hope to the younger generation at the Amsterdam Conference in 1939? Has it not long since faded? Has not the ecumenical operation become merely a part of the ecclesiastical machinery, one aspect of the ecclesiastical 'establishment'? Has not the World Council of Churches produced a far too comfortable situation for the churches, one which allows them to join in the ecumenical movement without at the same time incurring any obligations by so doing?

It was inevitable, of course, that the ecumenical spring should have been followed by an ecumenical summer, lacking much of the earlier freshness. For my generation the ecumenical movement had all the attraction of something unexpected and extra-ordinary. For the present generation it is simply part of the church's design. But is this enough to warrant the conclusion that the movement has become so institutionalized that it has practically come to a standstill? I believe not. Obviously the World Council has institutional features. But these are not necessarily signs of degeneracy. The World Council has to be an institution in order to do its job. Without a constitution, without common rules, without committees, without a staff, without a budget, all sorts of things can be started but without these things the movement cannot advance and assume a form sufficiently firm to enable it to help the churches to understand their ecumenical responsibility and to achieve a common witness and action in society.

If we want the end, we must also want the means to achieve that end. If our purpose is to help the churches to achieve a life of genuine solidarity and fellowship, of mutual stimulus and creativity, of practical co-operation, then we must also be prepared to create the necessary network of instruments to keep this process of common life moving. If we want an ecumenical instrument which is not just a pious dream but really enters into man's ordinary, everyday life, then we must also seek to make it visible and palpable enough to be taken seriously as a party to the dialogue in the interplay of the forces which actually shape the world in which we live. I offer as an example of this the field of international affairs. Certainly the World Council of Churches has not achieved what it would like to have achieved in this field. But the far from negligible concrete results which have been achieved—in the field of human rights, the Test Ban Treaty, East-West relations, the ending of the bloody civil war in Sudan—would have been impossible had we not represented an important section of public opinion and in our Commission on International Affairs created an international agency sufficiently competent to contribute to the discussion in the world of international politics.

The really astonishing thing is that people who want to see an active ecumenical movement addressing itself to the world should at the same time be opposed to providing it with an institutional form. For it is simply naive to imagine that conviction can influence what happens in the world without any need to find expression in concrete institutions.

But institutional paralysis can take other forms. A movement can, for example, be so taken up with asserting itself that it increasingly neglects to carry out its real and original task. Is this what has happened to the World Council of Churches? Certainly not in such simple terms. In the ecumenical field the choice is not between institution and task but between different aspects of this one task. In the many critical situations we have been faced with in the history of the ecumenical movement, the question has constantly been: to what extent must we give priority to the task of maintaining the fellowship between the churches, and to what extent to the other responsibility of bearing clear witness against injustice? During one of these frequent crises I put the matter in the following terms: the World Council has a special responsibility to maintain the fellowship between its member churches, for the achievement of this fellowship is the real *raison d'être* of the World Council. This fellowship is still young and extremely fragile. Clearly we must do everything we can to keep it in being. But it is a fellowship based on common convictions and called to common witness. An important element in the very substance of our fellowship is what we have hammered out together in our assemblies. Yet it is not enough to express this in the form of general principles; it has to be applied concretely in specific international crises.

Each new situation confronted us afresh with this dilemma. Sometimes we were unable to speak because we were not sufficiently in agreement. Sometimes we spoke at the risk of a breach in the fellowship, as in the case of South Africa. What cannot justly be said is that the determining factor in our decisions was always the desire to preserve our existence as an institution at all costs.

This is the place to deal with a question which is often raised, especially in the Netherlands. Does not the real weakness of the World Council of Churches stem from the fact that (to quote from a recent article) membership of the World Council imposes no obligation on the member churches? The question shows that the questioner has not understood the nature of the World Council of Churches. The World Council itself has never suggested that membership entails no obligation: on the contrary, a term which constantly reappears in World Council statements is the word 'commitment' which means precisely the acceptance of a real obligation.

How has this misunderstanding come about? The answer is that the World Council—in this is its originality, the new way it points—does not think of this obligation in legalistic terms as an obligation which could be enforced. A legal obligation on the churches would imply a central authority which can enforce obedience. Had it thought of the obligation in those terms, the World Council would have become an over-institutionalized super-church. Anyone who considers it a great mistake that the World Council should respect the autonomy of its member churches, should have no power to compel the member churches in any way, should take its decisions in a democratic manner, has already, wittingly or unwittingly, opted for a centralized instrument of power. In this present age when centralized institutions in every field, ecclesiastical and political, are finding themselves in a blind alley, do we really want the leaders of the World Council to issue instructions to the churches? Long experience has taught me that to take that way would get us nowhere.

The First Assembly of the World Council of Churches in Amsterdam unanimously adopted a resolution disavowing any idea of creating a structure dominated by a centralized administrative authority and declaring that the Council's purpose was that of a decentralized fellowship embracing considerable differences in church order, liturgy and forms of evangelism, and held together not by a directing

44

centre invested with legal authority but simply by the common confession of one and the same Lord and by the common task: in other words a pattern of great flexibility and freedom, in which the institutional element is secondary and subordinate because the desire is to restrict that institutional element simply to what is needed for the fellowship to live and operate effectively. This was the new factor introduced into the history of the church by the World Council.

But what precisely is the obligation of the churches? In drafting the plan for the establishment of the World Council, William Temple gave the following answer: 'The Assembly and the Central Committee will have no constitutional authority over the member churches. The only authority of the Council will be the weight it carries with the churches by its own wisdom.' We have always taken this to mean that, while each church must assume full responsibility for the degree to which it is willing to accept World Council statements, no member church can be relieved of the obligation to give serious consideration to the common testimony of such statements and to ask what specific obligation the testimony implies for its own life and work. To put it another way: *de jure*, this autonomy is *de facto* revitalized in the common life of the ecumenical movement, since the decisions arrived at together influence the churches in a way they cannot in the long run escape.

Addressing the Central Committee in Rochester in 1963 I made the same points in these words:

'Membership in the WCC implies that each member church gives serious consideration to the results of common study and discussion as these are expressed in reports or statements by the Assemblies or other organs of the Council. Each church remains free to disagree with any statement which comes from the Council. But all churches are asked to give serious attention to such statements, to decide whether they contain such "wisdom and truth" that they may be regarded as having a spiritual authority (for they cannot have any other authority) and, if the answer is affirmative, to make such statements their own and to apply them to the life of their churches.'

There is authority, therefore, but not the kind of authority which asserts: 'this is true simply because I say so and because of my official position.' Rather it is the authority which says: this insight has been granted to us; examine it and see if it convinces you too; if it does, then put it into practice'.

It is my conviction that this concept sets us on the right road to finding a more spiritual and more effective answer to the problem of common decision making. It would be wrong and in any case impossible for us to return to a situation in which any church body, however representative it might be, could claim to have, *a priori* and as a matter of course, an authority which exempted its decisions from scrutiny. It needs to be stated quite clearly that unity, common witness and co-operation are possible without everything being dictated from the top. It is in this way that the World Council must and can be the school in which we rediscover the genuine conciliarity which was a feature of the ancient church. The Russians call this *sobornost*, a way of living and working together in which all levels of the church participate. This will be an essential feature of the life of the coming *Una Sancta*.

It may be objected that this is pure theory. How does it work out in practice? If we take as the criterion the degree to which World Council decisions have been adopted by the official organs of the churches it has to be admitted that the results are very meagre. Smaller churches do not for the most part have the necessary machinery to implement many of the recommendations of World Council Assemblies. Larger churches are often too much taken up with their own problems. But is this the right criterion? I would say not. The real question is whether the main ideas about the task of the churches in our time, as these have been formulated in ecumenical statements, have made headway in the churches. To this question it is possible to give a much more encouraging answer. The attitude of member churches has undoubtedly been directly influenced by what the World Council of Churches has had to say, for example, about the solidarity of the churches which must find expression in mutual aid, the duty of the churches to help those in need, the responsible society, the position of the laity and women in the Church, the freedom of the churches vis-à-vis all ideologies, development aid, human rights, race relationships, and so on. And even in the most difficult field of all, that of church unity, the balance sheet is far from discouraging: the by now inevitable ecumenical nature of true Christian theology, the rejection of proselytism, definite progress in the matter of mutual admission to and recognition of the sacraments, a number of reunions between churches, a new encounter between the Christian west and the Christian east, the entry of the Roman Catholic Church into the ecumenical movement.

It is nevertheless true that a great deal more should have happened. But what has happened means that the World Council has succeeded in bringing into the life of the churches at least an element of dynamism. The same thing can be shown from another angle. If the World Council were never to be a nuisance to the churches, there would never be tensions between the Council and the churches. But in fact there have always been tensions of this kind. I recall the discussions on capitalism and communism during and following the Amsterdam Assembly, the role of the Council at the time of the Hungarian and Suez crises, the confrontation with the churches in South Africa, the Programme to Combat Racism. The very intensity of these tensions proves that the churches fully realize that membership of the World Council is no sinecure.

Moreover it was the World Council which in various ways put the question of the unhealthy growth of the institutional element in the life of the churches on the agenda. I recall the study of the non-theological (i.e. sociological) factors which hinder unity, the studies on institutionalism, the programme on the missionary structure of congregations.

In this connection I must also say something about the alleged bureaucratization of the World Council of Churches. It is asserted that whereas in its early years the Council was a personal and spontaneous operation, now it has taken on more the aspects of a bureaucracy. But a vage generalization of this kind is hardly much help. It is essential here to distinguish between different kinds of bureaucracy.

Sociologists tell us that bureaucracy means in the first place devoting time and energy to the production of useless documents and to vain discussions when they could be more usefully employed in other more immediately practical ways. I do not think it is possible wholly to exempt the men and women who work for the WCC from this charge. In this respect our staff are children of their times.

In the second place, the bureaucratic process means that the smooth functioning of the organizational machine becomes the top priority and there is less and less room for any new initiative for advance. In my opinion, no one who really knows the World Council of Churches can plausibly maintain that it suffers from this kind of bureaucracy. On the contrary, the problem is rather that the World Council produces too many initiatives which eventually come to grief because of conservatism or lack of imagination in the member churches. One has only to recall the proposals about development aid, about the Programme to Combat Racism, about intercommunion, all of which lead us a great deal further than many member churches have been willing to accept. Far from being composed of bureaucrats who seek to remain as anonymous as possible and who scrupulously refrain from advancing their own views, the staff of the World Council present an altogether different problem and many people in the churches often shake their heads at the temerity of the Geneva documents.

In the third place, bureaucracy can mean that in practice a group of officials exercise complete control over an organization and can no longer be checked by democratically elected bodies whose right and duty it is to take important decisions. Is this the case with the World Council? The danger is certainly not an imaginary one. Because of his work and his travels an ecumenical secretary can acquire an overall picture of the ecumenical scene and is therefore easily tempted to regard himself as the expert and to refuse to take seriously the criticism of church representatives with only limited ecumenical experience. But as the secretary becomes an even better ecumenical secretary he realizes much more clearly that his most brilliant notions and plans are worthless unless they can be communicated to and accepted by the member churches. Not only that. He also learns that Geneva is not the only source of new initiatives and that an important part of his job is to see to it that fresh insights from the congregations and the member churches are placed at the service of the ecumenical movement. Berkelbach Van der Sprenkel once wrote that it is a blessing for the ecumenical movement that there are not only church leaders who have their own local concerns and are at best 'also ecumenical' but also other church leaders who are 'only ecumenical'. The two groups need each other. It is my belief that the dialectic between staff and those who represent the churches is—despite difficulties—really practised and that it is therefore unjust to speak of a bureaucratization of the World Council in this third sense.

Is it really necessary for me in this connection to contradict the baseless assertion that 'the Central Committee is carefully chosen by the Secretariat'? Anyone who believes that should be condemned to sit through the long, wearisome sessions of the Assembly's Nominations Committee. He would there learn that the staff have no chance whatsoever of making the church representatives' decisions for them!

There is yet another criticism: does not the World Council seek to direct all ecumenical activities into official church channels with the result that all free and spontaneous unofficial initiatives are stifled? The answer is a very definite no. The World Council is far too aware of how greatly indebted it has been in its own history to the free ecumenical movement for it to entertain even for a moment the idea of any monopolistic policy. Among the people on the Central Committee and on the staff of the World Council are many whose first ecumenical experiences were acquired in the World Student Christian Federation, in the YWCA and YMCA. There is also a clear recognition of how much the World Council owes even today to the stimulus provided by such lay movements as the *Kirchentag* (Churchweek) and by other movements not officially connected with the churches. The disturbing thing to us is not that there are ecumenical movements outside the World Council of Churches. The disturbing thing is not the constructive criticism of sincere opponents, either. The only really disturbing thing is the attitude which writes off the official church ecumenical movement and regards it as something of the past.

I read in an article in the Dutch monthly 'Wending' that by becoming the concern of the churches, the ecumenical movement has landed itself in a cul de sac. The argument ran as follows: 'what kind of movement can be expected from institutions which have chosen to remain stationary, and none of which is prepared to risk its existence as an institution?' To this I reply that I do indeed expect movement from the churches. They have been moving during the last twenty years. I do not ask them to renounce their existence as institutions. Their task in the world can only be carried out adequately through their acting as institutions. I do however ask that they continually scrutinize the institutional aspect of their life in the critical light of their fundamental task to consider this aspect as an earthen vessel which needs constant re-adaptation to new assignments.

It is right that people should become impatient at the slow tempo of the official ecumenical movement. Those of us who have worked for a long time for the World Council are painfully aware of how frequently opportunities are missed because of visible or concealed brakes. We need the impatient people who call for boldness, imagination and forward-looking hope in action. But there is an impatience which gives up and an impatience which builds up. Merely to say no and to turn our backs on the existing ecumenical movement would be a desperate remedy and an act of sheer ingratitude. We have no right to throw away all that has been given to us in the movement in the past forty years. What we are free to do is to renew it, purify it and adapt it to present tasks.

What we need above all are men and women who will help us to discover the structures required in the radically changed situation in the world and in the Church. How can the World Council of Churches make the essential universality of the Gospel visible in forms that really point the right way? How can it ensure that the rich variety of spiritual gifts in the churches find expression in its own life and work? How can it demonstrate the Gospel word that Christians are never to be concerned for domination but always only for service? How then can it eliminate every kind of power politics and every kind of centralized direction and ensure the full participation of all spiritual centres? How can the World Council help the churches to crystallize soundly-based convictions on the great human issues and itself become the mouthpiece for these convictions at world level? In what ways are we to ensure that local congregations, the laity, women and young people all have a voice in the ecumenical dialogue and in decision-making?

The real question, therefore, is not whether it still makes sense to build ecumenical structures. The

question, rather, is the one raised by the apostle Paul
(I Cor.3:12): whether we are building with gold and
silver or with wood and straw.

THE ECUMENICAL WITNESS IN
THE RELIGIOUS WORLD

What should be the attitude of the ecumenical movement towards the non-Christian religions? This question was raised at the very beginning of the movement. For the Edinburgh conference of 1910 the answer was simple: evangelization and more evangelization. The continents which know the Gospel must bring this Gospel to the continents which still remain in darkness—it was as simple as that. But after the First World War, when the Christian world had lost a great deal of its self-confidence, it no longer seemed entirely self evident that from the Christian point of view the other religions could be considered as so much unoccupied territory. And while plans for the creation of a Christian ecumenical movement went forward, steps were also being taken for the foundation of an inter-religious world-wide movement. The famous pioneer in the history of religion, Rudolf Otto, created in 1921 a *'Religiöser Menschheitsbund'* (a religious league of mankind). He spoke of the desirability of a dialogue between the religions even then. Together they should create a 'world-conscience'. Rudolf Otto was supported by Friedrich Heiler who expressed the conviction that the Old Testament must be replaced by the Holy Scriptures of other religions for those followers of these religions who came to embrace Christianity. He also held that in the end all religions are basically one. Henry Atkinson, who had played an important part in the preparation for the Stockholm conference in 1925, organized a Universal Religious Peace Conference in 1928 with the aid of the funds of the Church Peace Union founded by Andrew Carnegie.

At that time the question therefore arose as to which way the ecumenical movement would go. Would it move towards a Christ-centred ecumenism? Or towards an all-embracing union of religions? Behind the proposals for the formation of an inter-religious front there lay undoubtedly the thought that the religious life of mankind must be saved through the co-operation of the great religions. This was also why the first Encyclical which the Vatican devoted, in 1928, to the ecumenical movement, described this movement as based on the error that all religions are more or less commendable because they all manifest in different ways the inborn tendency which leads man to God.

The choice of the real leaders of the ecumenical movement however was for a movement which had its foundation in the Gospel. Even though Friedrich Heiler was Söderblom's friend, and Henry Atkinson his collaborator, and even though Söderblom's field of study was the history of religions and though he was deeply interested in the great living religions, he refused to have anything to do with the inter-religious organizations. For the time being these organizations were unable to gain a foothold in the ecclesiastical world.

The problem continued to exist however. Did the rejection of syncretism really imply that there could be no collaboration between the religions? The world conference of the International Missionary Council held in Jerusalem in 1928 was largely dominated by this question. On the one hand people were deeply disturbed by the secularism which was encroaching from all sides. Everywhere the religions were being pushed back by the modern world with its science and technology which gave man dominion both over nature and over his own life. The question was raised whether the religions should not make common cause in this hour of danger. At the same time there was the much deeper insight into the spiritual life of non-Christians which had been gained through the science of comparative religion. Should the spiritual values which were to be found there not be recognized, and, if so, would that not change the whole orientation of the missionary approach? There were some people in Jerusalem, such as Professor Hocking, who gave affirmative answers to these questions and who expressed the hope that all religions, including Christianity, would be gathered up in one great world-religion. Others, among them Hendrik Kraemer, protested because of their conviction that the Gospel of Christ could not and must not be fitted into a general and abstract concept of religion.

A few years later this discussion flared up again, much more fiercely. In order to answer the question how the American missionary societies should tackle their task the so-called 'Layman's Enquiry' was held, under the leadership of Professor Hocking. The answer which emerged was that there should be a radical change of course. Where up till then the missions had maintained that there was only one way, the way of Christ, the new approach should be that the aim of mission is to bring the religious life of every nation to its full development. Mission should not be aimed at the destruction of other religions, but at their continued existence in order that all religions should stimulate each other in the unity of the most complete truth. From all sides voices were raised in protest against this new vision, including American ones. Toyohiko Kagawa's judgement, in Japan, was: 'This is mission without the cross'. I myself wrote a criticism with the title 'Mission without backbone'. But by far the most effective reply came from Hendrik Kraemer in the book which he wrote at the request of the International Missionary Council for the world missionary conference in Tambaram in 1938: 'The Christian message in the non-Christian world'. Kraemer based his argument on what he called 'biblical realism'. He refused to consider the Gospel as a partial truth which must be fitted into an all-embracing religious system. Christ is the norm and the crisis for all values and truths. This does not mean however that we look down on other religions, nor that we do not respect their spiritual life, or fail to listen before we begin to proclaim. Here Kraemer was in a strong position for no-one could accuse him of failing to study, with real attention, the life of other religions and civilizations. This had started in Cairo, where he had lived among the Islamic theologians wearing the fez, and under the name of Sheikh Kraemer. And he had continued in the same way in Central Java, in Bali, among the Bataks in Sumatra and in India. It was of course impossible to complete the discussion of Kraemer's books in Tambaram. But it could be said that the big stone which he had cast into the ecumenical pond continued to cause ever larger circles.

It was after the Second World War that two divergent developments took place. The Missionary Council and the World Council of Churches had continued to grow towards each other on the basis of a missionary theology which rejected every kind of relativism and syncretism, maintaining that Jesus Christ stands at the centre. The first regional ecumenical grouping in East Asia, gave priority to the common evangelistic task of the young churches in Asia. D. T. Niles of Ceylon, the leader of the East Asia Christian Conference, was indefatigable in his summons to the task of missionary witness. Bishop Newbigin directed the International Missionary Council in the same direction.

But during these years there were at the same time fierce attacks on the conduct of mission. These were based in the first place on the newly acquired cultural self-confidence of the now independent countries of Asia and Africa. The book 'Asia and Western dominance' by the Indian diplomat K.M. Panikkar is typical. According to him the end of the 'Vasco de Gama' period has come, the period during which the West could impose its will and its civilization on the East. This means that the period of mission has also reached its close. The attempt to conquer Asia for Christ has definitely failed in spite of the enormous protracted effort of the churches and the support of the general public in Europe and Africa. K.M. Panikkar could of course reach this conclusion only by equating mission with cultural expansion. His argument runs: Western imperialism is finished, *therefore* missions are finished. This view of mission was not only to be found in Asia and Africa—it gained more and more ground in the West. The Marxist description of the work of missionaries, as for instance in the Soviet Encyclopaedia, is of an undertaking to strengthen the position of the imperialist nations. Intellectual and literary circles in the West became fascinated by the spirituality of Eastern civilization, and so considered mission to be a primitive denial of cultural values.

Much more hurt was caused however by the blows delivered by the men who had been counted among the supporters of the ecumenical movement and who began to query every missionary activity. Professor Hocking completed his ideas concerning the merging of all the great religions. He visualized the birth of a universal religion in which the truths of all the historical religions would be incorporated. When that stage was reached the Christ-concept must be detached from the historical Jesus. Professor Arnold Toynbee, who earlier had put forward a Christ-centred concept of history, now reached the conclusion that Christianity should not just discard its 'Westernism', its westernized character, but should also renounce its traditional belief in the uniqueness of Christianity, because such a belief would create intolerance and pride. He appropriated the words of the Roman Symmachus spoken at the time of the defeat of Christianity: 'So great a secret may be reached by more than one road'. We must put an end to the particularism and the exclusiveness which have come down to us from the Old Testament.

At the time of integration of the International Missionary Council with the World Council of Churches in 1961, the missionary cause was therefore assailed by many radical questions which demanded answers. Moreover, some of these questions were raised within the Council, by the younger churches who wanted to remove all traces of Western tutelage and who demanded renewed reflection on the possibility of assimilating the cultural traditions of their own countries into the proclamation and the life of the churches.

The word 'mission' which in the past caused Christian hearts to beat faster, seemed to have lost a great deal of its glamour. And a new word put in an appearance, the word 'dialogue'. At the Fourth Assembly of the World Council of Churches, in Uppsala, in 1968, this was expressed as follows: dialogue implies a Christian approach to our fellow-men, which accepts them as persons and which is made in all humility. The Commission for World Mission and Evangelism began to organize meetings at which representatives of the various religions attempted to meet each other at a deep level. There is no doubt that this has led to all sorts of discoveries, as heretofore the parties had not listened to each other properly. The genuine Muslim or Buddhist is often entirely different from what we can learn about him from books. Prejudices have been exposed at these meetings. Conversations with Marxists have also been organized and have equally led to surprises. I am thinking of the conversations with the Czech Marxist philosopher Machovec who declared roundly that he had no time for Christians who did not try to convert him.

But what is the real purpose of such dialogue? Many different interpretations of dialogue seem to exist side by side. It seems to me therefore that it is useful and indeed necessary to identify and list these various interpretations. Six different types can be distinguished. Four of these would appear to me to be incompatible with the missionary task of the church and the nature of the Gospel, while the last two are entirely legitimate.

In the first place I would mention the dialogue which is based on the assumption that all religion is in essence a matter of subjective experience. Everyone must decide which kind of spirituality suits him best. In the same way as people choose in the fields of literature and art that which will provide the best stimulus, so they can choose in the religious field. There is at present a great deal of this eclecticism in which Yoga, Zen, visits to ashrams and an interest is esoteric mysticism each take their turn, or are tried all at once. This kind of dialogue is an attempt to enrich oneself with the insights and spiritual techniques acquired by the partner.

Secondly there is the dialogue which starts with the concept of the original religion of which all the historical religions are partial manifestations. The dialogue is used to search together for this original, universal religion. The differences and contradictions are emphasized as little as possible, because they are only temporary phenomena, while the core of the matter is that which can be found everywhere and at all times. Anyone who has been in contact with members of the Ramakrishna Mission in India will know the astonishing ease with which they reduce all religions to one common factor. But we in the West have also several movements which point in the same direction.

In the third place there is the dialogue which starts with the position that the time has come to found one single universal religion. Mankind can no longer permit itself the adherence to several religions, for this can only cause divisions. It is not denied that considerable differences exist between the various religions. But it is felt that these differences must disappear. Every religion can make its own contribution, but all will have to make sacrifices as well. This is syncretism in the true sense of the word. It used to be thought that syncretism was a typically Asian phenomenon. Nowadays we must admit that one meets it everywhere in the West.

In the fourth place dialogue can be based on the thought that the followers of other religions are really Christians, though they do not know this. This concept of 'anonymous Christianity' plays an important part in Roman Catholic theology and has also been defended by speakers at World Council gatherings. The argument runs: 'It is our task to awake the Christ who sleeps in the night of the religions'.

The mistake which these four views of dialogue have in common is that belief in the Gospel is considered as a special form of religion in general. Does the *homo christianus* belong to the species *'homo religiosus* ? In the era after Karl Barth and after Dietrich Bonhoeffer we can no longer assume this to be true. Barth made a sharp distinction between faith and religion. Bonhoeffer went further and said: 'to be a Christian does not mean to be religious in a special way..... The task of the Christian does not consist of reserving for religion as large a place as possible in the world, or over against the world'. And the great discussion about secularization points in the same direction. Arendt Van Leeuwen has shown that biblical thinking, by dethroning the gods, favours secularization, so that it is a great mistake for Christians to make common cause with the other religions against modern secularism and atheism. In this history of the missionary movement there are many situations where certain religious views or practices have had to be sharply rejected in the name of the Gospel, and certainly not because of a spirit of intolerance. Dialogue which is based on the assumption that Christianity must at all costs choose the side of religion *against* the non-religious powers cannot be defended either on theological or on practical grounds. One speaker in Addis Ababa referred to the 'universal religious community'. I find it difficult to attach any meaning to this concept. During my visits to India I have often had the feeling that I was more in sympathy with Jawaharlal Nehru, an agnostic who was sharply aware of the evil which had been roused by religion in his country, and who defended the rights of the oppressed, than with many religious leaders who defended the caste system or the system of purdah for women, and who remained completely passive in the struggle against hunger and poverty.

No dialogue at all then? I would not say that. There are forms of dialogue which are meaningful. There is first of all the dialogue which starts from the assumption that there are in this pluralistic world many tasks which can only be completed if people of every possible religious and even non-religious conviction are prepared to work together. Christians have for so long occupied a specially powerful position in the world, that they are still not used to the new situation, in which their voice is just one of many. We must learn to change our tune. This means that we must sit down with Muslims and humanists, with Buddhists and Marxists and Jews, in order to ask together which norms we can adopt in order to make the solution of the great problems of this world attainable. Discarding our dreams of a universal religion or even a universal ethic, we must have a businesslike discussion about the next steps which must be taken in order to find new and less unjust structures for the world economy, in order to find the criteria for a common stuggle against pollution and the exploitation of nature. All the religious and ideological families must learn that they cannot serve the world as long as they persist in their own monologue about their pious wishes for the future of society. The people who in science and industry, in government and in international organizations, draw up plans for the future and who often feel helpless, will only pay proper attention when the great religious and ideological families can agree on the specific steps which must be taken. I believe that we must give a high priority to this kind of dialogue which is concerned with these immediate, practical problems.

But there is more. There is dialogue which hopes to achieve a deeper level of communication. The Gospel is proclaimed by people to people. There must be a real encounter between these people. And that is impossible when one party considers the other simply as an object or as a victim. Both parties must be able to listen. And he who has come to say what he has discovered in and through the Gospel must give the example. He may only begin to speak after he has listened so carefully that he begins to understand how he can tell the story of Jesus to these people with whom he has come into contact, in such a way that it becomes relevant to their lives and can be understood in their situation. One of my Japanese friends, who has been a missionary in Thailand for many years, distinguishes between steamroller theology and water-buffalo theology. 'My theology here must start with the need of the small farmer, and not with the "Summa Theologica" of St Thomas or with the "Dogmatics" of Karl Barth'. The real missionary is not a crusader but a man prepared to let his world of ideas be crucified. And that is what happens in the dialogue in which the partner is considered completely as an equal, as a fellow-creature. It seems

66

to me that this was the way in which St Paul and St John listened to people in the Hellenistic world. How can we otherwise explain that they proclaimed the Gospel in a language and using expressions which are completely different from those of their own Palestinian background? They must have had many dialogues with the inhabitants of Antioch and Ephesus to be able to enter their spiritual world. It is not as if they have adapted the Gospel to such a degree that it has lost all its strangeness, its ability to shock. It does however mean that it is passed on in such a manner that the people of the Hellenistic world cannot reject it by shrugging their shoulders and saying that this is incomprehensible language which does not convey anything to them. We can say with Luther that the apostles had them *'auf's Maul geschaut'*—had learnt their idiom—and not just from a purely linguistic point of view, but also in the pastoral sense. They take the particular spiritual situation of their audience seriously. And they are not afraid in their proclamation to make use of insights and concepts which they find in the religious frame of thought of their partners, if these can serve to bring the Gospel closer. This is not syncretism, because everything continues to hinge on the original *kerygma*. It is good dialogue, however, because they have listened before beginning to speak.

There have always been missionaries who have studied the religious life of the people to whom they were sent with patience, respect and imagination. It is however also true that many of the young churches are still far too dependent on Western spiritual imports.

The task of ensuring that the Gospel strikes deep roots in Asia and Africa is one which we have hardly begun. And let no-one say that this task has become meaningless because all the old religions and civilizations are doomed to give way to the world-embracing technically rationalized civilization. It is becoming only too evident in our time that the old religions and the traditional cultures are not only very tough, but that they carry the potential for renewal within themselves.

We must now pose a question however which has received insufficient attention in the ecumenical discussion. Should we, in the present situation, only take account of the historical religions and of the ideologies which have taken on a clearly recognizable form? I believe that we must also look in another direction, which is that of the consciously paganistic religiosity. Though more difficult to identify, this is becoming a great power in our civilization, containing a much greater challenge to Christianity. This religiosity can be given different names. Johannes Huizinga called it the 'cult of life' and the 'obsession with life'; Jean Brun speaks of the 'return of Dionysus'. One could also say 'romantic vitalism'. The main thing is that it is concerned with the deification of life as such.

The prediction made by Marx and Freud, and much later by Bonhoeffer, that the end of religion had come into sight, has only partly come true. It is true that a modern type of man has evolved who, because he considers man to be totally independent, so that any talk of transcendental or superhuman reality is no more than a childish illusion, rejects all forms of religions as a sense of dependence (*'Abhängigkeitsgefühl'*, Schleiermacher). Jacques Monod the Nobel prize winner, in his book *'Le Hasard et la Nécessité'* despatches all religions, philosophies with a metaphysical dimension and Marxism with its attempts to give an objective meaning to history, to the museum for antiquities. The book's great success proves that for many of our contemporaries all religion is no more than an illusion.

But does this really mean that we have landed in an era without any religion at all? I do not think so. Just after Marx had completed his major book, a young professor made a prediction which pointed directly in the opposite direction. That was Friedrich Nietzsche. In his first essay *'Die Geburt der Tragödie aus dem Geiste der Musik'* (The Birth of Tragedy from the Spirit of Music), 1871, he described the conflict between the 'Appolonian' and the 'Dionysian' elements in Greek culture. Apollo represents reason and Socrates is his prophet. Dionoysus represents the untamed, explosive, primitive lust of life. Nietzsche drew a parallel with the modern world. He believed that this world has gradually had enough of the Socratic 'thirst for knowledge'. The Dionysian spirit is slowly reawakening. And he burst into cries of joy: when the want of Dionysus touches our tired civilization everything is changed; a whirlwind chases everything which is effete, the time of Socratic man is past; let us put on the ivy crown and take up the thyrsus.

This prediction, made a century ago, has also come true. The religion of life has gained more and more ground. In America its great prophet was Walt Whitman. Johannes Huizinga called him 'immensely primitive and pagan'. Then there was D.H. Lawrence who put forward the same thesis in all his novels: our civilization and society have suppressed the natural aspects of life, have cut it back and outlawed it. We must return to the primitive world. We must rediscover the old fertility religions.

Nietzsche came later to the conclusion that Apollo was not the greatest enemy of the Dionysian life-cult. In his last essay he exclaimed: 'Has no-one understood me? It is Dionysus against the crucified one'. And in his novel 'The Man who died' D.H. Lawrence depicted Christ meeting, after his resurrection, a priestess of Isis, and coming to the conclusion that the true life is the earthly life which comes up from the blood. It is curious and typical of our spiritual short-sightedness that there has been such an uproar about D.H. Lawrence's 'Lady Chatterly's Lover' while no protest was made about 'The Man who died'. Does this mean that it is an offence to call sexual matters by their proper name, and no offence to make a frontal attack on everything that is holy to the Christian?

National-socialism subsequently made use of this life-religion in a chaotic and eclectic manner. The Dutch theologian H. Miskotte drew a masterly sketch of this in *'Edda en Thora'* which appeared just before the Second World War. His aim was: 'to recognize in the new human type which seems to be making itself manifest in the totalitarian state a variant of the old, "eternal" man, that is to say: the pagan'.

After the life-cult had been taken to its ultimate and absurd conclusion, it might be expected that the religion of blood and soil would lose its attraction. But no, in so far as the modern novel, drama or film seem to have any overt or concealed message, it is that of the by now rather boring story of the suppression of spontaneous living by Christian moralism and puritanism, and of the glory of the discovery of the sparkling life of the body and of nature. In the socio-political field this vitalism has now taken a turn to the left, leading to the rediscovery of anarchism which finds its origin in the creative force of spontaneous, unbridled life. Herbert Marcuse has succeeded in interpreting Nietzsche, Marx and Freud in such a way that all three of them contribute to a revolutionary ideology which is to liberate the erotic energy of the instincts of life from the prison of the repressive consumer society. After centuries of suppression we must learn to accept life as an end in itself without any compunction, and reject every morality, every structure, religion or philosophy which have denied Eros his chance. We all know how these ideas have influenced the greatest protest movement which had its culmination in 1968. That we are here concerned with a religious phenomenon becomes quite clear when we examine the so-called counter-culture which not only hippies, but also various groups of modern artists and intellectuals are constructing over against and alongside the prevailing culture. In his book 'the

71

making of a Counter-Culture' Theodore Roczak shows how eagerly new religious experiences are sought after. The search is carried out in every possible direction: in the Far East, but also among the Red Indians and the Eskimos. The same question is put everywhere: who has fathomed the secret of the original, untamed, natural life most deeply? The distaste of the replete, artificial, technocratic society and in particular the new awareness that we are really engaged in a war against nature, thus destroying our earth, bring grist to the mill of the prophets of the return to nature. Thus we find ourselves in a situation in which religion, the death of which has been predicted, is in fact taking a powerful revenge. It seems to me that the question of how the Church and Christianity will meet this challenge has become the central problem of our witness. We have failed to take this new religion, which is at the same time so ancient, really seriously. We have thought that Nietzsche's ideas were no more than the product of a sick mind. We only discovered national-socialism when it was too late. And when Hitler's time was finished we expected that the West was bound to resume its Christian tradition. And even now there are many who consider all this life-religiosity as a quaint fashion which will no doubt pass. But the new religion has taken too much hold, it responds too well to all kinds of needs of modern man. We must take it seriously, whether we like it or not.

What does this mean here? It certainly does not mean that we must say: 'Thank goodness that we have new allies in the struggle against atheism. Now we can recover from the fright which Bonhoeffer gave us when he said that we would have to proclaim the Gospel in a world without religion'. Why should we not say that? Because this would mean that we have failed to understand that this religion is not simply a non-institutional religion outside the church, but that its very essence is pagan. To proclaim the Gospel to people who worship strange gods is not easier but more difficult than to proclaim the Gospel to people who have no gods at all. It is naive to think we will find an ally in the life-religion. In his book 'Honest to God' Bishop J.R. Robinson merely shows that he has understood neither D.H. Lawrence nor Bonhoeffer when he considers them as spiritually related because both look for the transcendent in a world without religion. In fact Lawrence seeks to bring the old primitive religion back to life, while Bonhoeffer demands that the faith be freed from the embrace of religion.

We will have to learn again how to recognize paganism. Paganism is not the same as atheism. Paganism is the worship and the service of the powers which rule the natural life as long as this life follows its own road. Paganism is to worship life itself instead of the Creator and preserver of life. Can, or should the church have a dialogue with this neo-paganism?

The answer to this question must certainly be: yes, in so far as dialogue means: to listen to each other. For we have a lot to learn here. Instead of saying disdainfully that these new pagans have just warmed up to an idea which had been overthrown centuries ago, we must ask *why* the old religiosity has revived itself with explosive force in our day. It then becomes only too clear that Christianity here has to face an old debt which has never been paid. For both the church and theology have paid hardly any attention to the questions which the prophets of the life-religion seek to answer. What do we as Christians have to offer in the field of theology of the natural life (which is entirely different from that of natural theology)? Why did the churches not warn long ago against the *hubris* of modern man's attitude to nature? Why have we waited so long before facing the question of whether the deep mistrust of Eros in Puritanism was really founded in the Bible? In short, why have we allowed things to come to such a pass that the caricature of Christianity as the negation of life is better known in a wide circle than the Gospel of the renewal of life?

But after we have heard these accusations and drawn from them the necessary conclusions concerning the reform of our thinking and speaking, then we must also say emphatically that the religion of life and faith in the living God are totally incompatible. Everyone must make his choice here. And this is indeed the choice between Dionysus and the Crucified One. We are back here in the Old Testament situation of the prophecy against Baal and Astarte. No alliance is possible in this case. For it is a choice between salvation and perdition. The issue is this: can man really attain *shalom* (peace) in a surrender to the life-instincts, or does this *shalom* only come from the God of Abraham and Isaac and Jacob, the God of Jesus Christ? The issue is whether what is in fact our society's contempt for nature should be overcome by the deification of nature, implying a new slavery, or by the reverent acceptance of nature as creation and gift, for the use of which we owe God an account. The issue is whether we allow ourselves to be swept along by an Eros who has gone wild and who destroys every real human relationship of trust and charity, or whether we give to Eros his proper place in the light and the service of the Agape.

It seems to me that it is high time that the ecumenical movement issued a rallying cry to the churches in order to strengthen them for the great spiritual struggle about the final meaning of life, a struggle of world dimensions and which therefore must be fought by the churches together. With one accord we must proclaim to the world which is searching for life, that it cannot manage without the God to whom we can say: "With Thee is the fountain of life' (Ps. 36:9).

SHOULD THE ECUMENICAL MOVEMENT FOLLOW THE AGENDA OF THE CHURCH OR THE AGENDA OF THE WORLD?

The ecumenical movement has never been just a family party of the Church, with the world left out. The first big church conference of the movement was that of Stockholm in 1925 and the main topic there was the task of the Church in the world. Nathan Söderblom was convinced that there was no time to lose. He did not yield an inch to those who warned that the churches could not give a united witness about the social and international problems if they had not reached theological and dogmatic agreement. His answer was: the situation is so urgent that we cannot wait; we must act as if we have already come to a complete agreement. He took it into the bargain that the theology which had been chased out by the frontdoor, had crept in again through the backdoor.

There were really two theologies in Stockholm, which got into a real struggle. On the one hand there was the so-called 'social gospel' which was defended not only by the Americans, but also by the English and the French. Its founder, Walter Rauschenbusch described it in terms which sound remarkably modern in our ears: 'Humanity is waiting for a revolutionary Christianity which will call the (present) world a bad world and which will change this world'. For it is 'the real purpose of Christianity to transform human society into the Kingdom of God'. As can be seen: the accent lay on the horizontal aspects of the Gospel. Jesus was first and foremost the great reformer of social relationships. This social Christianity was based on a strong belief in the progress of mankind. History was on the move and the powers working for equality and brotherhood were invincible. The whole social and international order could be christianized. Over against this there was a theology which considered the Kingdom of God as a purely eschatological concept, another world which will replace this world at the time appointed by God; this theology, which was mainly defended by the Germans, took a deeply pessimistic view of the possibility of bringing about any considerable social change.

The Stockholm Conference was not really able to overcome this polarization. The theological confusion of tongues was too great. But Stockholm at least managed to affirm that the churches must recognize their duty to put the Gospel into practice in every sphere of human life: industrial, social, political, international—and for many people this was an entirely new affirmation. It also meant that social problems were discussed in a very concrete manner. Archbishop Söderblom for instance declared himself clearly in favour of the eight-hour working day, in those times a very progressive view. The question remained unanswered however as to whether really basic change was possible if the social structures remained intact, or whether the churches ought to fight for a radical change of those structures. The sharp challenge which Marxism had put forward or the questions which the freedom movements in Asia and Africa were beginning to ask, still met with little response. It was hoped that the new international bodies such as the League of Nations and the International Labour Office would solve the great problems of mankind. It was the task of the churches to give these organizations 'soul'. One of the concrete results of the conference therefore was the founding of an International Christian Social Institute which would help the churches in the reflection on their task in the social field and which would collaborate with the International Labour Office, where representatives of the governments, together with those of the employers and the workers, would work out the new social order.

During the years after the great economic crisis of 1928 however the world began to change rapidly. 'The world' no longer meant the nations who, with the signing of the Kellog Pact in Paris promised to outlaw war, and who now at last had begun to negotiate disarmament in Geneva. The world now meant: Mussolini, Hitler, Stalin, the Spanish Civil War, Ethiopia and ever-increasing unemployment. What should be the attitude of the churches in this kind of world? It could not be one which implied that the society with which it had to deal was still largely christianized and only needed to be christianized a little more. For it now became only too clear how near the surface paganism was still to be found and how easily large sections of this Christian society submitted to the totalitarian powers. The churches were forced to ask fundamental questions about the foundations of society, in order to take up a position against the idols and to rally people in order to rediscover the biblical vision of the common life. This presupposed however that there was a church which knew what it wanted and which did not live in such a symbiosis with the world that it became impossible to know where the church ended and the world began. In this way there came about a searching and questioning as to the identity and integrity of the church. The struggle of the church in Germany illustrates how much the church needed this new reflection on its nature. Even in America, where Reinhold Niebuhr had prepared the way, a group of young churchmen published in 1935 a book with the shocking title, especially in America, 'The Church against the world'. Richard Niebuhr showed in the introduction how the church had adapted itself far too much to the world and now must learn again to speak independently. One sentence, which John Mackay had written in a memorandum for the Oxford Conference, was picked up everywhere because it expressed exactly this desire for a real church, dedicated and obedient to her task: 'Let the church be the Church'.

This did not mean at all a withdrawal into a clerical ivory tower. In the 'Student World', in those days practically the only forum for international ecumenical discussion, there was a great deal of radical social criticism. Here Niebuhr, Nicholas Berdyaev, Paul Tillich, E. Rosenstock-Hussey, Denis de Rougemont and the men of the French Esprit-group attacked the structures which had to a large extent become rigid and rotten. And there was J.H. Oldham who had begun with the preparations for the Oxford Conference in 1934, and who, like Diogenes with his lantern went round looking for the men and women who could point out the new roads towards a radical renewal of social and international life. He managed to mobilize sociologists, politicians and economists so that Oxford 1937 was much more representative and relevant that Stockholm had been. Instead of limiting itself to the concern to penetrate the existing order with a Christian spirit, the conference attempted a critical examination of the structures and institutions of society. The Oxford message to the churches reads: 'The forces of evil against which Christians have to contend are found not only in the hearts of men as individuals, but have entered into and infected the structure of society, and there also must be combated'. And the conference reports on 'Church and State', 'Church and Nation', The Church and the Economic Order', 'The Church and International Questions', treat these acute problems more concretely and more critically than had ever been done before on the ecumenical level.

Then came the outbreak of the Second World War. For a number of churches this meant a choice between either becoming a confessing church, prepared to proclaim the sovereignty of the Lord in every sphere of life over the pagan ideologies, or denying their very calling. Even if they did not address the world as clearly as they should have done, they nevertheless gave a new witness, in coming to grips with the real world. The Church had become part of the history of man again. A great deal of work was also done during those days towards the formulation of a common witness of the churches concerning the post-war social and international reconstruction. The words of the German Evangelical Church leaders in Stuttgart in 1945: 'that Christians had not been courageous enough in bearing witness' really applied to all the churches, and it was now realized that this failure must not be repeated.

And so we arrive in the post-war period which has brought new chances for the churches and in particular for the ecumenical movement. The World Council was inaugurated in Amsterdam in 1948. The first Assembly devoted considerable attention to social and international problems. J.H. Oldham's proposal to adopt the concept of the 'responsible society' as a criterion for the social task of the churches met with general agreement. With the criterion it became possible to tackle all the main issues simultaneously. The implication was that everyone must be given a chance to share in the responsibility, to make everyone accept the responsibility for his fellow-men. Moreover, society should not be considered as an end in itself, but should be subject to norms of eternal validity. All this meant a strong emphasis on the rights of man. The ecumenical movement took a critical attitude both towards capitalism and towards communism because in neither are the three dimensions of the responsible society realized. This was an extremely uncomfortable position during the cold war, as both parties considered the ecumenical movement an untrustworthy element. Not just the independence of

the movement was at stake, however, but also its
integrity, for it must show that it was the common
task of the churches to sound their specific note in
the confused struggles of ideologies and power blocs.

There was in those days much talk of the
function of the Church as watchman. Was the
implication, consciously or unconsciously, that the
real leadership of the world belonged to the Church?
Not necessarily, because the watchman can interpret
his task as the modest one of the sentry. It is true,
however, that in that period, which saw a revival in
the life of the churches in many countries, great
expectations concerning the role which the churches
could play in the reconstruction of post-war society
were cherished.

Experience from earlier years had taught that
nothing is achieved by general declarations issued by
ecumenical gatherings, if they are not followed up by
attempts to work out concretely the practical
political conclusions which must be drawn from these
declarations. A Commission of the Churches on
International Affairs was therefore instituted,
consisting of specialists in the international field, and
with a secretariat which works full-time on the acute
problems of international life. Thus the churches have
their own lobby at the United Nations and with the
governments. The main aim here is however not to
defend the interests of the Church, but to contribute
towards the solution of the great problems on which
hinge the peace of the world. In the social field too
there was a shift towards more concrete forms of
action. The studies on rapid social growth in

countries of Asia and Africa brought together economists, sociologists, politicians and churchleaders in order to work out guidelines for the building of the social and political order.

Can it be said that these attempts to exercise a direct influence from within the ecumenical framework on the social and international life, met with any results? It is difficult to give an answer to this question. The important decisions in politics are nearly always the result of an interplay of forces. And who can say how much has been contributed by this or that participant. I think however that we may, quite soberly, draw up the following balance sheet. First of all: there are the many cases where the churches have not been able to take action because they found it impossible to define a clear, common position. Secondly, there have been many cases where the recommendations or the warnings of the churches met with no response because the governments were not prepared to pay the price which would have to be paid for a peaceable solution. Thirdly, there have also been a number of cases where the word of the churches formed an important contribution to the formation of an international public opinion, which in turn made it possible to take new and constructive steps along the road towards a better international order. Presently I will give some concrete examples. This balance sheet is certainly not impressive enough to create euphoria. But it is a balance which should not be neglected in any assessment of the work of the ecumenical movement.

About 1960 however a fierce debate got started

on the question of whether the ecumenical movement ought radically to change its attitude towards the world. Many people were deeply disappointed that the wonderful plans to renew society through a renewal of the Church had come to nothing, or almost nothing. It looked as if all the attempts to affect the genuine reforms had run aground. There was a strong desire to get rid of the established order, which seemed no more than disorder. Should the task of the ecumenical movement in the world not be ruthlessly re-examined? A new language is introduced by the new generation. There must be an 'exodus' from the institutionalized churches which are too closely involved with the 'establishment'. The aim should be a 'secular ecumenism' with the service of mankind as its main purpose. (This is not the same as a secularized ecumenism.) What is needed is a theology of revolution. It proved to be a confused debate: the old and the new problems became entangled. Let me therefore begin by referring to those questions which are no longer really relevant, or which should no longer be relevant because they have been answered adequately in the course of the history of the ecumenical movement. First of all: does the ecumenical movement have the right and the duty to make pronouncements on social and international problems? To this I reply with the question: should this still be a problem today? Nearly fifty years have passed since the new beginning at Stockholm, and have we not learnt together in these years the lesson that to reduce the Gospel to a matter between God and the individual soul is a denial of the prophetic witness of the Old and New Testament? Has the ecumenical consensus reached on this matter really penetrated so little into the member churches? The old song of the Church which is only concerned with the salvation of the individual has become more of a lullaby in these days. From every side, not only from the critics of our culture, or even from the hippies, but also from the representatives of science and industry come loud proclamations that our society, based as it is on production and consumption, is on its last legs and that only a new ethic can save us from catastrophe. Should the churches at this critical moment withdraw into their shell and assert that their Lord has nothing to say about the struggle of mankind to build a meaningful community in which man can lead a life that is worthy of him?

A second question, which is not really relevant, is: Has the ecumenical movement really taken the great social and international problems of our time seriously? Repeatedly one can hear the assertion that only in most recent years has the ecumenical movement fostered a real interest in social problems. Such an assertion can however only serve as proof of a lack of knowledge of the history of the movement. One of the main causes behind the origins of the ecumenical movement was precisely the dismay over the impotence of the churches to give a clear common witness on social questions. And from Stockholm 1925 and Oxford 1937 until the World Conference of Church and Society in Geneva in 1966 and the World Council of Churches' Fourth Assembly at Uppsala 1968 the common struggle to evolve such a witness has continued. It may be said that the results do not come up to the expectations. It cannot be said that people have not worked with energy and passion in this field.

A third irrelevant question is whether the ecumenical movement has not limited its concern to the motives and norms which ought to govern the life of the Christian in society, thus neglecting the problem of the justice of the structures. Anyone who has taken note of the pronouncements of the Oxford conference of 1937 and in particular of the Assembly in Amsterdam of 1948 will know that it was understood from very early on that it was not just the social attitude of the individual Christian which mattered, but that questions about structures were of utmost importance. What is the concept of the responsible society if it is not used as a touchstone from which the existing structures must be judged? Since Oxford 1937, but even more since Amsterdam 1948, the criticism of the existing social structures has increased both in clarity and in content.

A fourth question, which is equally superfluous, is whether the ecumenical movement has not occupied itself with social and international questions in a merely verbal manner, and in the form of vague generalizations, and whether it has ever taken a tangible part in the struggle for social justice and lasting peace. It is a fact that much ecumenical activity in this field had taken the form of general resolutions and reports. It is also true that many of those pronouncements were too vague to have any *direct* influence on the outside world. One must however beware of underestimating the significance of a consensus of the churches in the socio-ethical field, which can serve as the basis for local, concrete decisions. The ecumenical movement has however learnt more and more that it is of no use to confine itself to generalities. In consequence it has, especially since the Second World War, taken sides with regard to many burning political issues on which the well-being of mankind depends. It was possible to do this without ignoring the realities of political life through the collaboration of expert laymen.

Has this had any results? There is certainly no reason to exult over the successes of the ecumenical movement in this field. But there is equally no reason to pretend that all the efforts have been in vain. I mention just a few instances of interventions of which we can say in the light of objective evidence that they have achieved real results: the influence of the reconciliation in Stuttgart (1945) between the churches on the reintegration of Germany in the international community; the effective collaboration in the formulation and acceptance of the Declaration of the Rights of Man; the contribution to the termination of the Suez conflict (1956); the support of the preparation and accomplishments of the Treaty of Moscow concerning nuclear tests (1963); the initiative to persuade the rich countries to put a fixed percentage of their income at the disposal of the developing countries; the creation of the ecumenical atmosphere which made the *'Denkschrift'* of the German churches on relations with Eastern Europe possible, which in turn exercised an important influence on the formation of public opinion in Germany; the services rendered in reaching the peace treaty between North and South Sudan. These are tangible results. To these must be added the interventions which cannot be publicized because they would harm the good cause. I do not give these examples in order to sing the praise of the ecumenical movement, but in order that everyone may form his own judgement on the basis of the facts.

However, though we can answer a number of critical questions by simply referring to the actual history of the last forty years, there still remain other, less critical questions which have received no answer at all, or only an inadequate one. In recent years some very pertinent questions have been raised which it would be wrong to avoid. Again I mention four.

In the first place: Is it not true that the churches are to such an extent involved in the present social order that the ecumenical movement lacks the freedom to be able to speak prophetically? This is a question which we cannot lightly ignore. It is indeed true that the churches are tied to their social environment by so many different ties that their witness is either restrained or seemingly unconvincing. There are silver cords which may tie the Church either to the state or to some social group. There are ideological cords which link the Church to a bourgeois mentality. It would however be wrong to conclude from this that the ecumenical movement and the churches lack the right to speak. For the liberation from the prison of worldly powers comes exactly at the point at which the churches demand again their independence and learn to speak out freely from conviction of their duty. And in this field there are well-founded reasons for hope. The encounter and the conversation between the churches, leading to mutual correction, has the effect of teaching the churches to see themselves as others see them. The ecumenical movement serves here as a movement for the liberation of the churches. A new confidence develops when the churches take warning from each other and learn to consider their own task in the perspective of the world-wide task on the *Una Sancta*. It is simply not true that during the last thirty years the churches have merely copied the voice of surrounding political and social powers like parrots. I would remind these critics of the role of the American churches with regard to the war in Vietnam, or that of the French churches with regard to Algeria, or again that of the West German churches concerning the relations of their country with Eastern Europe. There still remains a great deal of work to be done to make this liberation movement effective in every field. But a beginning has been made.

A second pertinent question is: Is the ecumenical movement not too optimistic about the possibility of gradually reforming the existing order (or disorder)? Does it not live too much under the illusion that the great problems such as the relation between the rich and the poor countries, exploitation, racial discrimination, the abuse of power by the big powers, can be solved without breaking away entirely from the present order? Has the movement become too pragmatic through a desire to evade generalities? I want to make four remarks in reply to this very valid question. Firstly: even such great revolutionaries as Lenin have underlined repeatedly that it is pointless to make propaganda for an immediate revolution in situations which lack the conditions necessary to bring about such a revolution. Secondly, revolution implies violence, and Christians can only accept violence when all the other possibilities have been exhausted, and even then they must do everything in their ability to check the demoniac power of violence. Thirdly: one cannot make generalizations here: every continent, every country has its own particular historical situation in this respect. What applies to South America is not necessarily valid for Asia or Europe. Fourthly: the ecumenical movement must be prepared to work both for the great radical transformation of the social and international structures as well as for the modest reforms which can be made immediately.

The next question which has not yet received a sufficient answer is: has the ecumenical movement laid so much emphasis on the life and future of the *Church*, that it has failed to give sufficient attention to the questions concerning the life and the future of *mankind*? Was the movement too taken up with the agenda of the Church to take the agenda of the world really seriously? It is of course a fact that the ecumenical movement, faced with the heavy task of bringing the churches, isolated as they were from each other, to co-operate together and to lead them along the road to unity, has had to give a great deal of time and attention to the problems of interchurch relations. Often I have sighed when the world situation forced us to interrupt the work of building up the ecumenical movement in order to pay attention to this or that critical international situation. But this was not because the internal politics of the ecumenical movement seemed more important than international politics. It was really because only a basically coherent ecumenical movement, founded on convictions which were substantially held in common, could have anything to say to the world. Must we turn the Church inside out? Alright, but if the lining of the coat is all torn, turning it inside out is not going to be of much help. There is a time to gather together. And there is a time when the exodus must be made. Both belong to the essence of the Church.

The last of these pertinent questions is whether the ecumenical movement, even if it has not acquitted itself too well in the socio-political field, has in fact shown itself to be on the side of the poor and the oppressed. It is well that this question has been formulated so sharply at this time. The fierce discussion about the ecumenical programme to combat racism proved that we are here faced with a radical choice. I consider this programme as an unavoidable consequence of everything that we learned together in the ecumenical movement. The manifestation of disinterested solidarity speaks more clearly than any ecclesiastical declaration. And it has been a joy to me that in Africa this has been noted with gratitude, mixed with surprise. People had not believed that the churches could summon the courage and the imagination to come to such a decision. And one unexpected result has been that with the new credibility which the ecumenical movement has acquired in this way, it has become possible to play a determining part in the termination of the long and bloody civil war in the Sudan and in the reconciliation between the combatants in that country.

It is clear that in the new situation which has been reached because of the developments in the Church and in the world, it is no longer sufficient to repeat the old formulae, but that we must find new answers to the new questions. I would however like to say something more about the perspective in which we must view our task.

This perspective must be a prophetic one. This is so because the only specific and distinctive contribution which the Church can give the world concerning the social and international order, is the prophetic witness as it was originally proclaimed in the Old and New Testaments. A well-known saying of Karl Jaspers about the chances of the Church could be adapted in this way: All the chances of the Church with regard to the world lie in prophetic witness.

Why should this be so? Because prophecy knows of a dimension of human life which the world does not know of itself: the dimension of God's actions. Prophecy bears witness to that which God has done, to what God does and to what He will do.

Permit me to quote a few striking sentences from the Dutch theologian A. Van Ruler: 'Our knowledge of history which comes to us through prophecy is not an insight into history, but a knowledge about history. The jungle in which we find ourselves is not cut down, but an open space is cleared where the sun penetrates, to our comfort. ...And besides, apart from this clearing, paths are made for us between the tree trunks and through the trailing creepers, along which we can go. Besides the promises about God's actions, prophecy contains the commands for man's actions. ...And we receive just enough to see the next step: the path through the jungle is cleared before our feet.' Put differently: in a world which comes up against closed doors at every turn, prophecy is the word which breaks through and which opens up new perspectives. The prophet Micah expressed it thus (2:13): 'He who opens the breach will go up before them, they will break through and pass the gate, going out by it. Their king will pass on before them, the Lord at their head'.

Through this revelation of God's will and of God's marching orders prophecy takes up the struggle against the three falsifications of the religious life: against the 'private' piety which wants to reserve God for the individual soul and which denies God's dominion over the world; against the religious institutionalism, for which the overruling concern is the continuity of the traditional forms of the religious life; against the idolatry which makes worldly powers, systems and ideologies into absolutes.

This war cannot be waged by drawing up general principles. Neither the Old nor the New Testament offers us a system of ethics. The prophecy is couched in extremely concrete language and speaks of actual events. Beginning with Amos, and until Jesus, who is more than a prophet, the social ills and sins which lead to exploitation and estrangement, are called by their names. Unfortunately the churches have during their history not given the prophetic witness the attention it deserves considering the central place accorded to it in the Bible. For long periods the churches have neglected to pass the prophetic word on to the world, leaving it to its own fate. It is therefore understandable that there is at this time again a strong movement afoot to draw the attention of Christianity and of the Church to the world and its needs. The real question however is now whether this movement is a genuine revival and actualization of the real prophetic tradition. It certainly contains a number of elements of that tradition: the rejection of an egocentric, private piety, criticism of the self-assured religious institutions, the struggle against the powers which are a menace for mankind. But are these elements held together in the right context? In the original prophecy this context is always the revelation of God's will. It always begins with: 'Thus says the Lord'. In the second letter of Peter this is expressed thus: 'Because no prophecy ever came from man's initiative. When men spoke for God it was the Holy Spirit that moved them' (Jerusalem Bible). Is this realized sufficiently in the attempts made to bring Christians to play a relevant role in society? Again and again I get the impression that in much of what is written or said about the social function of

94

Christianity we are offered an uprooted or partial prophecy. Uprooted because there is so little evidence that the writer or speaker is moved, overpowered, by the personal encounter with the living and speaking God—while it is this encounter which renders the prophecy truly significant. Partial because under those circumstances the insight and the breakthrough have disappeared from the prophecy, while only the commandments remain.

The point is not whether the churches are too little or too much involved with the problems of the world. Basically they can never be involved deeply enough. But the question is whether they are involved in the right way. Is it in the manner which Martin Buber called 'theopolitics'? Or in the manner of half-Christian, half-worldly ideology? We are impressed by the insights given to us by the human sciences, and quite rightly. But not even the best sociology can help us, if we do not live out of our own deepest source of strength. Are we not in the same plight as Hagar and Ishmael in the desert? They nearly perished from lack of water, until they noticed that there was a source near at hand: the complete prophetic proclamation. If we could listen to this together, we would lose every desire to waste time over polarizing discussions. Then our agenda would indeed be the agenda of the world, but not in the sense that the Church is only allowed to answer the questions about the world with which she is occupied.

When I hear it said nowadays on every side that the ecumenism which is only concerned with the Church is finished, and that the only relevant

ecumenism is that of common social engagement,
then I recall the crisis which hit the ecumenical
movement in 1932. At that time there was also a
great tension between 'orthodoxy' and 'orthopraxis'
(the right practice). Then there was also the question:
unity of doctrine or unity of action? Dietrich
Bonhoeffer, an extremely young man at the time,
made two speeches to show the way into the future.
First he pointed out that there was a great confusion
of ideas. He thought that the cause of this confusion
lay in the insufficient theological roots of the
movement. At an ecumenical youth conference he
exclaimed: men of action must cease to disparage
theology. As long as we are uncertain, he said, the
ecumenical movement will be the prey of every trend
appearing in the life of society and politics. The
ecumenical movement did not just exist to carry out
common social tasks. The ecumenical movement is a
specific manifestation of the Church, which is
concerned with no more and no less than the
rediscovery of the true task of the Church. This task
consists in the proclamation of the presence of Christ
in the world. It must be made clear to our society
how Christ is our peace. But the word of the
contemporary Christ consists of Gospel and
commandment—these two cannot be separated.
Christ is the Lord of the whole world. The point is
that we must hear the concrete word which Christ
gives to us in our actual situation. In this way
Bonhoeffer transcends the false choice between the
alternatives of an ecclesiastical and a worldly
ecumenism. An ecumenical movement which is *only*

interested in doctrine remains in the air. An ecumenical movement which is *only* concerned about action loses its identity as a Christ-centred movement and so becomes a tool of the forces which are drawn up against each other in the social and political field.

It goes without saying that there must be social engagement. And of course there may, nay there must, be co-operation between men of goodwill of every kind who come together on the basis of this concern for justice and peace. But that is not an alternative to the gathering of the scattered children of God. Social engagement is the necessary consequence of our becoming the church-together.

It is my belief therefore that the ecumenical movement can only have a future if it avoids the temptation of choosing between the unity of the Church and the unity of mankind, and instead learns to realize more and more fully that the Lord gathers his people in order that they may be a light to the world. There is a future for the ecumenical movement provided it does not cease to reflect on its true *raison d'être*, and draws its life from the heart of the Gospel. Thus the movement will be moving forward. Then the Holy Spirit will work among the churches, taking us and our churches by the neck, driving and binding us together, and thus enabling us to carry out the renewing and saving task in the world.